Takotsubo

the journey of a transplanted heart

Jacqueline Haskell

Published by Cinnamon Press
www.cinnamonpress.com

ISBN 978-1-78864-161-6

British Library Cataloguing in Publication Data. A CIP record for this book can be obtained from the British Library.

Designed and typeset in Bodini by Cinnamon Press. Cover design by Adam Craig © Adam Craig.

Cinnamon Press is represented by Inpress.

Acknowledgements

The italicised lines in 'Foreign Body' are quoted from 'The Soldier' by Rupert Brooke.

'The Berlin heart', 'There are three hearts you can choose from:', 'Aria' and '*Takotsubo*' were published in Issue 52 of *The Bombay Literary Magazine*, August 2022. 'We are all in this together: the heart, the scales, the gods and the feather' was published in *Brittle Star*, Issue 48, June 2021. 'Complications' was published in *Locked Down: poems, diary extracts and art from the pandemic*, Poetry Space, February 2021. 'Alice like the wind', an earlier version of 'Queen of Hearts', won second prize in the 2014 FISH Poetry Competition and was published in *The 2014 FISH Anthology*, July 2014.

The italicised lines in 'There are three hearts you can choose from:' and 'So sorry for your loss,' are quoted from Dido's Lament ('When I am laid in earth') from the opera *Dido and Æneas* by Henry Purcell (1659 – 1695).

Thank you to Claudia Gould, Maria Jastrzębska, and Simon Barraclough, who all took a look at the manuscript at some point in the last six years; to Michael Forester—fellow writer and life partner—for never saying the poem was fine when it wasn't; and to everyone who's been there for me on my writing journey.

Jacqueline Haskell has an MA in Creative Writing from Birkbeck, University of London. Her first poetry collection, *Stroking Cerberus*, was published by Myriad Editions in 2020, as part of the Spotlight Books series for underrepresented writers. Her poems have appeared in *Atrium, Brittle Star, Dream Catcher, The High Window, Anomaly Literary Journal, Ink Sweat & Tears* and *The Broken Spine*, amongst others.

Her short stories and flash fiction have won prizes in numerous literary competitions, including the Bridport Prize and the Asham Award, and her debut novel, *The Auspice*, was a finalist in both the 2018 Bath Novel Award and the 2020 Cinnamon International Literature Prize.

Contents

To my mother, Sylvia June,

and my grandfather, Joseph Colbourne,

who made poetry one of my earliest memories.

the average adult heart is roughly the size of a clenched fist

and weighs about 11 ounces

We are all in this together: the heart, the scales, the gods and the feather

In the darkness, Christ climbs down from the cross, sets off towards The Field of Reeds (it will be a while before anyone notices he is missing).

He places his heart on the golden scale, watches the desert road, the shuffling of feet; watches Ammut (*such a minor god!*) as she licks her lips in anticipation of her dead.

Later, women come and find Him gone. They take down the cross, plant it in the valley filled with shadows, wait for spring.

Takotsubo

The Cabbage (CABG)

In which

you have a 'significant cardiac event' as they call it

you have a CABG to try and fix it

then a stroke under the knife

followed by an 'incremental hospital resource consumption'

and an 'outcome wait'

after which they keep you alive with a VAD
(ventricular assist device)

then they prepare you to die

Above ground

Afterwards
you become afraid

of the sun   of the daylight
everything

so you begin to walk at night
the pale blue silk of your pyjamas
slicing through
the long hours of darkness

without people the streets open up before you
the security lights on the roof of the shopping centre
flash bright and artificial, hot with fever

in the pet shop some kind of exotic bird
—crimson ivory grey—
flaps belligerently in its cage
beak nudging through the bars

destructive behind the grimy insides of the windowpane

you press your head
to the glass

the bird—already your beloved—
wheedling you to set it free

Matryoshka

'Jesus said thank you, you know, *before* each miracle,' says the hospital chaplain, coming up behind you and resting his hands on your shoulders. You smell the mint and eucalyptus, the antiseptic drops on his breath. 'Every time.'

Once the chaplain is gone, you sit for longer than usual, gazing up at Him. You scan His ribcage for the famous drops of blood, wonder if a transfusion might have saved him.

   We are like the woodcutter without wood, those of us who survive a stroke under the heart-knife, and we fill the rehab wards with the squelch of worry balls, the oversweet stench of our interiors clenching and dividing, our bodies imploding.

   Our eyes hawk those who ring the bell—adopted from the children's ward tradition—and leave, not yet knowing that once we are out, we will crave this place, where our dead-aliveness fits: the rigid ward campaigns, the workhouse humour, the endless ham and cheese sandwiches.

No privacy until night, when, in your hospital bed—sides up lest you should do further harm, *ha!*—you hear the shrieking outside your window that in the beginning you thought a fox, but now you're not so sure; now you imagine the town's youth on the razz, their cries reaching out to you through the rattle of the Tramadol trolley—*Thank you*, you say, *thank you*—come to uncouple your dreams.

Pumphead

Waking to the scratch of lichen and the fluster
of swifts in the eaves, you scour the small ads—
there must be other heart depressives out there!—
ignore the pain of swallowed grit and mutilations;
ignore their entrances and exits high above you,
the glimpses of their dust-bowl wings.

The empty nests, double-brooded,
their screaming-parties, that sickle-winged rollercoaster flight—
they never touch the ground, you know, those birds—
we'll share those twisted-dervishes, me and you,
that one complete aerobatic of the heart,
before we plunge to earth, caught in the slipstream
of those white-knuckle kinkhead blues.

Nursemaid

How they fell into the ritual of keeping me alive with that kind of nervy, alienating, obviated intensity; with those around me—motherfatherwifelover (in the end there is no difference)—wishing for my death and plotting against it in roughly equal measures; where they believed I didn't know; where they believed, all this time, that I was simply lost to good old pumphead paranoia; me, incapable of knowing which will kill—they or you, *dear heart*—how they trimmed their vowels, fell to discussing me in front of me.

The Berlin heart

This is how it happens: his heart, not on his sleeve but attached
to a backpack, strapped with two-and-a-half hours of batteries.
This heart that carries grief, waits
patiently for rain, the trickle-feed of the sun, plasma
shoals swimming for cover beneath his skin, blood, pumping,
the floor rushing to meet him. His weight, a fulcrum point
between sacral and solar plexus. The churr and chime
of the machine, batteries alarming the external workings of his concubine
(His dominatrix! *Sit near a power source at all times!*),
its third leg dragging behind him,
dredging black water
in its cut.

When it is gone, finally, this contraption,
he feels unmoored;
those days and hours, now irredeemable, waver
with the frailty of a ceasefire—
God's alarm clock,
set to some unknown glottal

stop
of the heart.

There are three hearts you can choose from:

1. your own diseased heart—final outcome guaranteed
2. beating transplant—the longest wait, outcome uncertain
3. non-beating 'heart in a box'—journey time (donor to
    recipient) up to 8 hours
    (*This last will increase your chances, notes his surgeon, in the
    margin.*)

He casts aside this missive, future-paces to his funeral,

— *Remember me,*
Thy hand, Belinda, darkness shades me

On thy bosom let me rest
More I would, but Death invades me

jots down the order of the service, underlines the salient points.

— *Death is now a welcome guest*

He underscores this last, again and again;
multiple slashes of violet ink swim the pages of the aria
(which he guarantees will be out of tune),

— *When I am laid, am laid in earth, May my wrongs create*
No trouble, no trouble in thy breast

the organ drowning out their timid voices,
pigeons swelling the chorus—
but oh! that descending chromatic fourth—what an opener!

Aria

His voice overwintering;
the tinkle of consonants on ice,
a lifetime of syllables, frozen in place.

That aria perched in his vocal folds,
notes scattering in his throat—his tongue,
a silver heron above his spittle-stream—mid

-sentence and he is done.
He returns to his violin, levitating above
the pressure points of his collarbone,

but that too is without refrain.
There is nothing of its notes in him,
just the stickleback trajectory of the heart:

that beat, his breath, the alchemy of his phrasing,
the steady fastness of strophic ghosts—
he could no more speak than pull a trigger.

Roadkill for the shadowman

a splayed
red-tailed hawk goes down
beneath the wheel

no one slows or gets out to look

the hunter now the kill

no one stops when you collapse
behind the wheel
concertinaed on the bypass

The widow

In which

she remembers their childhood
makes love to his post-operative body
becomes accustomed to the hospital
attends a séance
takes an African grey to a funeral

When you were a child

you wore your heart outside of you,
plastic piping Play-Doh'd to your chest;
doctors and nurses wriggling under the table,
feet tangled in the spare sheets,
(I still have that photo, stethoscope stuck determinedly in your ear:
I can hear your brain beating, I said.)
but always you were cured.

iota-eta-sigma

With one thrust he enters her, his weight upon her,
the jagged surprise of him,
her savage colours—magenta, cobalt, cassel earth—
beating through her brain;
her startled lips parting from her thoughts,
her fingers, heavy still with paint—
everything that once flowed from her brush
now curdling at her touch.

He says they're numb, his scars, stretching him tight as the
wound   gut   of   the   *del Gesù*
his sheet music—the Bruch—lying untouched, ever since.

And at the window, the moon,
the palest curling sliver of a moon;
a divided moon that ghosts
and thins and flattens them
as the night-house creaks around them,
faces as notations,
pressed together on the page.

How to make yourself at home in the hospital:
a relative's guide to survival

She finds that she enjoys this, this living here; the smooth swish of
the floor polisher in the early hours; the sirens, their blue lights—
someone always worse off (although she hates herself for thinking
it)—swirling around her like the drop of petals. In the corridor, the
night leans towards her, takes a breath. Waiting room lilies
incandescent in the gloom, their blooms conspirators in life and
death. *No flowers on the ward*, as if even they could not survive.

He could come at any time

She knows this;
in the way she no longer touches him,
resists assurance that it's okay to get on the bed.

Above his head, machines glow traffic-light crimson, green, burnt
ochre,
leads jump-starting each breath. His case notes perched at his feet,
the small print: so many words for blood.

His sheets, cool and pale, she holds the linen close, not him.
There were nights when she held him, of course there were,
just not here, not now.

As if from another room, she hears the whistle and draw of his breath
expunged from his body. Both of them, afraid; the ragged bob of pain,
the darkness never far away.

Next day, she stays home, removes the cat from his nest in the airing
cupboard,
intent on sharing a little of her misery, folds and refolds inherited
linen,
corner to corner, dust to dust.

He could come at any time, the ferryman.

A tourist in her life

She wraps herself in her Great-Aunt's bedspread—she of the quilting bees and breakfast gin—each square emblazoned with the cross-stitch of the heart.

Would they be too old-fashioned at the wake, she wonders, the antimacassars across her best chairs? She worries about the ham and cheese sandwiches dripping pickle, the awkwardness of spinach vol-au-vents, discreetly picked from teeth. The sourness of cheap funeral wine—will she have time for communion, beforehand?—her regrets spilling wafer-thin, pale as aspic.

Repenting yesterday's cruelty, she makes another lunge for the cat, catches him by the scruff, and, rendering him immobile, bundles him back into the cupboard. She tries to keep his claws away from the Irish linen and manipulates him into her oldest blanket, into the warmest, smallest space, and, ancient as he is, he lets her, until even her touch becomes too much, and he hisses, green-eyed, blinking with a forest of reproach.

Finally, she shuts him in, leans back against the door jamb, and hears not his mewling, but the cries of gulls on the industrial railings of the old chain pier; that first night—an out-of-season weekend, their first together—waves breaking beyond brackish water, hair made anemone by soft Welsh rain. Until a sudden ache in her breast robs her of the memory, leaves it all used up, spread too thin, like the jam she used to make, her summers wild with the slippery paste of hedgerows, clotting cream on delicacies, too sweet for her new, austere palate.

False widow

Saw your herbologist in the supermarket today;
sudden rain, dust rising, drew her inside,
Pac-a-mac hastily erected over white
coat, a small child at each seam, scoring
smoothed-out floors with their sandals, little snails
slithering through the aisles.

Which bean? she held up two cans, pinyin labels
ragged, edges sharp as *Saola* horn,
the scene monochrome, grainy,
air-conditioned breath ghosting from her. She knelt,
so her boys could stab their choice,
blunt fingers clasping sods of rusk.

As I passed, she looked up,
the way she'd made you look up, into her light:
your pupils—no, just the one—contracting,
your head jerking, as if you saw spiders there.

Vital signs

I will get a tattoo, go to a séance.

If she mentions Beloved…

(you bought the bird, of course you did, went back in the daylight
of which you claimed to be so afraid)

… then I'll know, your brother tells me,
as we go inside.

I see ruffled feathers, a dove perhaps?
Yes, feathers—in a church.
A handful of fur, spit-aled breathing,
the comfort of lavender spaces.

An orchard, blossom falling…

On the way home, I dance the pavement cracks,
look for signs that you are here.

Dearly Beloved,

says Beloved, from beneath the covers of his domed and gilded travel cage (for Nick had so loved and indulged him that nothing was too good for that bird) currently occupying its own pew.

Nina—somewhat less indulgent—reaches across and taps sharply on the bars and wishes that she had listened to common sense and her brother-in-law and left Beloved at home—I mean, good God, who takes an African grey to a *funeral*?

Irritated with herself, she shifts on the dank stone pew, causing her handbag to jostle the nearby cage.

Fuck it! Screeches Beloved, unnerved at this sudden intrusion into his space.

Fuckity fuckity fuck it! He squawks, in a rhythm comfortingly reminiscent of freight trains on the railway tracks of home—a whole other world about which he'd quite forgotten until that moment – as Nina breaks the golden laws of parrot keeping (he had after all been Nick's bird, not hers) and pulls back the folds of his blanket to peer directly inside, make eye contact.

Oh, dear God, she whispers, shielding her own face behind the blanket, as if this very act would make her invisible to the rest of the congregation.

Abide with me, sings the choir.

God squad! Hoots Beloved, *Dear God, God, God!* Bobbing his beak in time with the words, thoroughly enjoying himself now.

Oh, good God, he echoes, more quietly, meeting her gaze with some sympathy, for he would have comforted her if only he'd known how.

So sorry for your loss,

they murmur to the widow, after the service.

No one says this to Beloved: even when the conure died,
no one but Nick thought of Beloved.

Thy hand, Belinda, darkness shades me,
croaks Beloved from the back of his cage.

As they talk, the aria rises and fades,
scratchy in the parrot's throat, G minor,
to a tune he has never heard,
from a service from which he was (forcibly) ejected,
but nonetheless remembers—in some detail.

'but ah! Forget my fate…'

Beloved, cataclysmic with grief.

The surgeon

he shaves

listens to Costello while he operates

almost orders chocolates

works on his lecture notes

puts a trace on his lover's phone

inherits a dog

Complications

knife crime   energy cap   GDP   modern day slavery

19

all this the surgeon hears before he shaves

at work
he scoops out a shallow grave
in the cavity of the heart

a
gaping
gasping
eradication

all
the while
his mind
circling

those keys on the table, that note,
the roof of his mouth closing on her words

Pump it up

He plays this during surgeries, he tells her,
not long after they first meet
—the routine ones, the stents, the balloon angioplasties,
where, he confesses, his mind wanders—says it reminds him of her.

She is not sure if she is alarmed, or flattered—
she doesn't *like* Costello even;

the Elvis though… that heartbreak hotel,
all those desk clerks dressed in black.

Vivisection

Long hours and the fetch of her keep him distant—heartsease (that old wives' tale) on their balcony in Andalusia; flamingos on her Spanish plain; the mesh of her latest sculpture as it takes wing back home in her gallery in St Ives: all of these are hearsay now.

His hand trembles, hovers in the cut; his team looks up, unused to this hesitancy.

Four hours in, he asks his registrar to close, rips off his mask, a speck of saliva cornering his mouth.

In the corridor, he pulls out his phone, Googles *Valentine Favours*; red icing sculpting the raw, dark chocolate of apology, just like the Love Hearts of his youth:

SWEET HEART

LUSH LIPS

BE MINE

His hand hesitates over the button: *Place order.*

Trick or treat

He jiggles his goddaughter and his lecture notes on his knee with roughly equal enthusiasm. *And on his farm,* he croons. Ela looks up at him, a second—no, make that a third—generation too late.

Running a finger down the page, he traces distant chronology... *Year 7 anatomy, cost £1.50 per heart materials. Place the organ in the dissecting pan, rinse off the excess preservative...* to next week's inaugural lecture, across the pond: Cedars-Sinai.

Out comes the highlighter, already leaking fluorescent onto his cuff. *E-i-e-i-o...* he sings, louder, but still she blanks him, waves a piece of wooden farmyard jigsaw in his face—a cow's udder, a suggestion of hind quarters—while diagrams of zebrafish, salamanders, turn pink in his hands: they who can regenerate the heart throughout their lives.

And this latest study, the pig's heart, *that trick or treat chimera!* He wants to tell them—Ela, his students, anyone who will listen—that there is hope; he wants to tell them that it is not cruel, this werewolf derivation, that this *is* hope. That we can survive the chickens and the monkeys and the blame.

Baa baa! Moo! Ela puts the piece of wooden jigsaw in her mouth. He wants to tell them they will do no finer thing than this.

24-hour trace

He slumps against the old sea wall,
legs askew as though fallen

                from height,
toys with his mobile, slides the apps

                  back and forth
releasing jingle after jingle into the briny air

inhaling cormorant and kittiwake

                their cries
harvested by the surf; too far gone, like him,

                unattended

                in the mermaid-shallows
he combs the apps for sign of her return,

puts a trace on her phone, a GPS to her heart.

The laying down of scalpels

Later, he gets home to a kitchen sterile as his operating theatre, peers into rooms he has not seen in daylight since they viewed the house, when he'd nodded in each doorway, one hand fingering his pager.

In the back garden, he steps over the big brute of her dog, who cowers at his approach, even now, two years on, whimpering with every flutter of house martins in the eaves, every flash of carp in the netted pond, decking streaked with his big brute piss (Surely she can't have left him the dog, when she has taken so much else?).

He pauses outside the glasshouse, its panes spectral in their delicacy, glittering, webbed panes, threaded with creepers and deceit.

The heart

In which

the donor heart
journeys to its destination

Pacemaker

A woman
on a blind bend

A woman
jogs on cobbles
bends
to examine a nail in her sole

A driver
blinded by the needles
of a sudden ice shower
brakes

A woman
on a bend
hits the windscreen

Imago

The heart,

its pupal, intimate with air and fog,
carries she-feet over cobbles,
unaware it will—abruptly—

have no place in her skin
(But ahh, it was such perfect skin!),

The heart,

sinks to the frosted earth with her,
absorbs the heat and light of her,
waits for her morning breath to obey.

Bosporus

Sirens slack and silent, the medi-van parked up by the river,
its surface skin on milk in the early light.

The drivers slouch outside it, crescent men with cigarettes and
Turkish coffee, foaming sweet and dark as blackstrap.

The muezzin calling them, the shadow of the minaret,
the *iqama* summoning the line for prayer.

Passports waiting, stamped, visa'd, ranged in order,
their own hearts beating, careless of the task.

Death hand

White van men of the cross
gambling while in line for the border,
steely foreign clouds obscuring the dawn.

Inside, he—the travelling surgeon—
holds Hickok's cards: two black aces two black eights—
worst of all, this time, even his kicker cannot save him.

Outcast

Passing through tollgates
for which we have no change,
we are turned back from Pazarkule.

The long road. Headlamps, dense
upon the tarmacked plain, throw speckled light on
glued and misted songbirds.

At the camp, he enters me illegally
with the slash of backstreet knives,
pastry cutters slicing the soft-flour heart of you,

excavating your narrow-skeined arteries, damming
plum-coloured rivers; always there is force,
ever are we compromised

as the hands of the white-gloved
magician vanish you from me,
and the initiated palm their coin.

The cold caravan of the heart

Outside,
the call to prayer,
the smell of spices, sour from the Souq.

They think I won't remember:
this journey, these men, these cards;
the talk of ice-cold storage, all redundant now.

Recording the conditions of an emergency,
this box, my non-beating-ness,
they think I won't remember.

The recipient

In which

Alice wakes at an unexpected moment

is put in isolation

discovers rejection and broken hearts in outpatients

has a conversation with her transplanted heart

acquires a taste for coffee

considers her sins

Anticoagulant

Although she knows she should be out of it, she hears them;
hears the sounds of traffic four floors down,
inhales sharply each time they make the cut.

A white van, a milky river: she dreams of Istanbul
—a place she's never been—an unlit fire,
two black suits, marked cards.

The surgeons take a break, leave the sternum,
a walnut cracked in half. She panics, eyes taped shut.
What if they abandon her like this?
Victim to a sudden amnesia? A seizure of their own?

Awake again, she scans their countenance for clues:
the paper gowns, the anonymity of masks,
Joker adversaries hacking away inside her.

Avalon

Slot hunger through the cracks; waft
the smells of vernal grass and honeysuckle; crush
sand shells from the ocean, their conch backs broken by the tide;
let silverfish slither on damp sheets from this wettest of summers.

Throw in your heroes, *Le Morte d'Arthur*, knight by man,
sand them down and push them beneath the door:
the King, Launcelot, Guinevere, Merlin—all who mattered then—
until you too are on the verge of dawn.

Bring salt, that you might season these last hours with them;
your shadow too, that it might keep you from the sun,
time-out from this whole rarefied dynasty, your days
opaque as Nimue below her watery Avalon.

Fashion daisy chains, their escape ropes coiling underneath the
door;
the ward sister, hovering, impatience barely concealed, eager
for the next empty bed. *Take off your mask and gown*, follow the
signs:

This way out.

Queen of Hearts

Breathe, commands the woman,
Alice breathe!

somewhere inside
the tongue of my old-black-dog licks me clean,
black-dog lips, black-dog clean

in this transplant-wonderland where all
and nothing is as it seems

in the corridor we meet, post op,
framed against the ghost-green paint
that gives us both the look
of being under-water

she, head-down to her clipboard,
charting her daily list of breathers,
she, with her white-rabbit smile and sagging scrubs
hurrying…

me, in the waiting room,
where my chest awaits its turn,
numb and cratered, its long bright zipper
scissoring me out of yesterday's dreams

The Stand-in

First time out alone
the breath takes in the lungs
hauls the
heart
along with it

Strange new landscape
rising
falling
inside her

The sensation on the road—on
each and every road—that she has
a nail in her shoe

Can she survive this archaeology,
shake off these barren fields,
this wrong side of the tracks?

Foreign body

There was someone else before you, okay? There, I've said it.

Look, you don't know me—I understand, really I do—
I could list my habits, good and bad, past misfortunes recollected.

A pulse in the eternal mind, no less
See, I've been studying your war poets
(they're not a touch on Hikmet though:
his little girl, ashes on the wind,
scattered velvet from her bones...)

And think, this heart, all evil shed away—
do you know this line? I bet you do.
Say we at least have this in common?

Give me a chance, huh? This is a foreign field for both of us...

I can't bear rejection, never could.

Re: Exit Strategy

Dear Heart,

What do I have to do to make you want to stay?

I did so much to get to know you—even ate from your communist syllabic Hikmet, drank bitter blacks from *canephora* beans: the crust, the wet aroma, my pores steeping in your cup.

I cannot allow that you would choose to leave me—*am I nothing to you?*

When did you learn to mistrust me so?

Even the space between your beats is unreliable now.

Yours ever,

Alice

Aftertaste

Coffee, dark grounds foaming in the pot; she craves it constantly,
sweet and bitter, like nothing she's ever known,
it will not leave her.

She tips the pot, spreads the grounds,
where once she read the leaves:
I see a tall dark stranger...

She grips the plunger:
The Hanged Man holding tight onto The World.

Curious Alice,

waits no longer for her life,
breaks her own fragrant membrane with her fingers,
she, with her one-way rabbit hole,
the heart—*her* heart—vanishing

the moon practising above her,
nearing its strawberry solstice,
daily nightly deathly
in the undergrowth

no, not you Alice, never you; you
were never there with us to raise a cup,
never present—
always too big or too small,
too Alice

You never saw them Alice, the blossoms, the fruits of your orchard
traversing the veins to your heart, upwards from your empty ground

Fast furious Alice

kneels to dark men in bad alleys,
unlaces boots in far-slung frontiers

those men, the last one—the one she might have loved,
had he let her—
naked in his suit, so shy, so full of dollars,
his sperm brushing her cheek like cumulus-heaped
detritus, hands in her hair,

-         *Come on, darlin', come abide with me—*

waiting on the dawn.

Her only crime,
the hot wet necklace of those dusky dreams.
(Oh Harry, ever steadfast Harry!
You were my breadcrumbs through the woods—
how I should have loved you for it.)

It's hard work this not sleeping, the constant watching,
the flash of hunters in the night.
She cannot tell if Harry too has lied, or if it is all her,
an error of perspective.

Pearling

Harry stalking; Alice, kicking off her shoes,
the track stony—marram grasses, dunes

hovering above dark water; herself,
a wading bird, skirt coiling around her ankles

until the tide sucks her down, seaweed gravity,
head bobbing, deep into the waves

where, dolphin-like, she locates the others, the
soft pale others, the ocean's insomniacs

feeding on her waste; plankton
searching out the muscles and the tissues of

her pelagic avatar,

she listens for their pulse through water,
eavesdrops on the faintest echolocations of her heart.

The scar tissue

In which

Harry laments the new heart
mourns the lost Alice

And what is it, the heart?
It is the sound of the pine breeze
There in the sumi painting

Ikkyū Zenji, Zen master (1394-1481)

Harry cannot

love her, cannot love the new heart.

Cruel and surprising this—
he doesn't want her—it—in his dreams,
the very whoreness, the blowsy-ness of her.

His living ghost,

the seep of his grief,
plugging the gap beneath the doors and
the windowsills of his gingerbread house,
towels tight against this Gorgon's rage.

Harry shuffles

through the places that they knew,
strength sapping. Blue cliffs edge his forest,
a cracked pond, crocodile ice:
entwined hearts girdling,
the killing of a branch to fruit the tree.

Aconites

He considers another appeal, though he can't see it doing any good: it has been too long. She-of-the-lost-heart will have no memory of him, no understanding.

Please come back, please—just as you were, he'll say, in the voice he used only for her.

Outside, a sudden shower, icy pellets thundering into the garden: hail in April, turning to snow.

He thinks about the last time he saw her whole, in the hardly-yet of early spring; all around them her aconites massing, their willingness to flower before everything else. Inscrutable, stubborn.

Come Christmas, he will pack up their house and leave. When he lifts it from the soil, the *Eranthis hyemalis,* he will find the ground curiously a-shimmer, a tiny patch of golden leaf, an ephemeral, shallow-rooted, tubers just below the surface, but pure and perfect, as if the sun's rays have planted themselves there.

Moon, voyager

Black blood, mulching underfoot,
always on the cusp of her,
the tiny sequoia kernel that she'd become.
Branches pruned of emotion,
he cuts one to hide himself
though the thought roams through his body
that he will find no comfort here.

A thousand origami Dunsinanes pass through him,
he lifts an arm, axe flailing.
Then the ivoried sight of her restores him:
her hair, candyfloss, the flutter of her,
the press of ashes, and
above him, a Steller's jay,
beneath a stranger's moon.

Takotsubo

The heart is its own idiom,
its own dark horse;
starvation in the anterior distribution,
your wooded body its one and only country.

The heart seeks its own asylum,
beats blood for your father and mother,
your chilled alabaster brother,
a true rose of lokma, challenging its own eviction.

Sequoia

In which

Alice goes into the woods,

hears the Homeric Hymn to Aphrodite,

rejects both lover and heart;

does not return

Sequoia 1

It is winter. You sit shivering under a clear, cold sky. All around you the redwoods loom close. Last time you came, you left your blanket, now it is lost beneath a compact spray of snow, its exact location defying your prodding and poking, fingers scrabbling with the claws of a forest animal.

You are too tired to search further; you take off your mask, sit under a clear, cold sky. It is nearly midday. Still you come in daylight, so that you will not be missed, so that you do not have to find your way home in the dark.

Sequoia 2

*So that you do not have to find your way home in the dark, you stay
close to the road, venture only into the first, smallest enclosure, feeling
your way into the strange new landscape.*

*This is because you are frightened; you have acquired separation
anxiety: from life, from Harry, from your heart, its non-beating-ness;
you, who now have only moss and sorrel for company, cavernous root
systems thrusting dirt into the air, bark peeling, nymph-sap bleeding
songs into the earth; you, skirting iron-watered dew ponds, mirroring
seed cones, herds of black-tailed deer drinking from their depths,
feasting on tanoak sprouts.*

*Everything is twice your size suddenly, even the foxgloves, silencing
the movements of hunters stalking prey.*

Sequoia 3

Stalking prey, Harry in borrowed waders, in the seep of his grief, sucking in the autumn mulch the first time the two of you came here, you, a disciple of one, keeping close, intimate with air and fog.

Although the forest covered many hectares, you felt exposed, slithering, lurching across crumpled trees, forest-fodder weighted with fungi; ground already transformed by a far-off summer, a clutch of pink campion thriving underfoot.

But for now, all you have is this light, these woods, a sudden glimpse of deer, barely there, then not: even this is uncertain.

Sequoia 4

Even this is uncertain; you have long since lost your way.

'This is it,' says Harry, coming to such an abrupt halt that you almost fall.

'They're all around us now: I can feel them,' he says. This exact spot painstakingly chosen for the power of its earth and sky, the inter-connecting ladder of trees, the spaces between their trunks, the hamadryads, a sacred geometry of belief.

You yourself feel nothing, just the cool silence of the place, the occasional pitch of sunlight on your shoulder.

You have no reason to believe you are near to the tree, your tree, your sequoia—you see only the clumsiness of Harry's search, the way spores shimmer and scatter before him, soft on broken twigs, two serpents shedding skin, the extinguished bonfire of a life—but your gaze travels the distance.

Sequoia 5

Your gaze travels the distance, your fetid breath is returned to you. It is the dank, dismal rot of this place that burrows deep into your chest, your heart vanishing into the undergrowth.

The gentle thud of your whistle, hanging from your neck, now salivad over, then, sharp and keen, a daily taunt to a succession of wayward hounds loitering in the shallows of Reep Pond.

These memories pull you through the spindle of your days, though now you can see their thinness, the very brittleness of your life, how Hansel and Gretel it was—is—coming here; only you are the villain, not the hero, and you do not have the luxury of breadcrumbs to guide you home.

Behind you in her tea-cake house, the witch burns blind, and so do you.

Sequoia 6

The witch burns blind, and so do you; the old drabani, *from across the cut, she warned you many times.*

A bird, wild in the house, a harbinger of death, she said. Always.

That is how it began, you, unexpectedly breathless in its chase (already suspecting the need for doctors, waiting rooms, an ECG): a bird, wild in the house, on that day, when you did not wake fully, though you occupied the same space, the same air as those around you, you were never fully present.

Although you were still there, a part of you entered the forty-nine, right then, although your breath still stained the windows, misting panes.

Sequoia 7

Your breath still stained the windows, misting panes.

Before dawn, the dream of a foreign field. Your body, shivering, dizzy, inhaling sharply, an anvil pressing on your chest; your limbs unsteady, phantom in their betrayal.

Harry moaning in his sleep, a tall dark stranger.

Outside, a Hunter's Moon. That early snow, a fatal darkness; the drip of your heart's melt.

Nestled in the attic beneath a blur of down, Harry misses you.

Where are you, Alice?

Sequoia 8

Where are you, Alice?

You crawl inside the memory, always too big or too small. Draw it to you, upwards from your empty ground.

The penknife, an unlikely present for a girl back then, trying it out for size, the shape and feel of it in your teenage hands. The first cut is the deepest *reeling endlessly in the youth club hut—thirteen-year-olds trying desperately to know the world—and that knife, incongruous, ivory, turning in your pocket; your hands all heat under the still-scratchy Christmas-present parka. Frost and slivers of yesterday's ice underfoot, each trunk planted square, precise, a far-flung, regimented enclosure.*

You pick the tallest—do not yet know it is a sequoia. At home, you will look it up—in Latin it's Sequoiadendron giganteum, in the family of the Cupressaceae; dawn, coast, and giant; their brittle wood shattering upon falling, they become fence posts, shingles, matchsticks, even. At thirteen, this waste means nothing to you.

A rush of air, an owl plunges through the canopy; spinning around, you watch wings brush branches, showering hoary particles, a whitened owl—beckoning you to its wild nocturnal ways.

You run your hands over the bark, fibrous, furrowed, flick the blade (its first time open).

Sequoia 9

Flick the blade, its first time open, begin to cut the bark: two hearts entwined, girdling it to an early death.

It taunts and beguiles you, this cutting. You cannot help but hope you will see the ferns underfoot again, smell the vernal grass and honeysuckle, before you cannot walk that far.

Each walk, ever shortening, you practise the eulogy of your existence. In the beginning, its sparseness startles you; you cannot account for the years, other than in dog-time; a small teaching job; Harry, of course; no roots but these, running like skeletons beneath you, their branches interconnected; some first lines; early drafts, all unsuitable for publishing, their spent pages, the obscurities of your being, leading you here, where you might consume your life, like the children in the pot, cannibalised by those who love them, famine seeping through their bones, settling deep inside your heart.

Sequoia 10

Deep inside your heart you story-tell the myth of the land, passed on to the new knowledge-holders; each word a cut tunnel between fallen trees, the light bleeding out, slicing through the long hours of darkness, each déjà vu another tale, a new part of yourself, the rib of Adam replanted; the ancients, laid bare to the eyes of strangers round campfires, eyes straining white into the night, blurring into one, because, like your griefs, they number many.

Sequoia 11

Griefs, they number many; when, finally, you come at night, they stalk you between trunks, with the stealth of a great, wild cat, its rictus grin, fixing you, your heart a saboteur inside a chest that shuns its beat. (What if they abandon you like this?)

The nocturnal forest is an altogether different place, more so than can be accounted for by the ooze of light, spillage filtering through blackness into the coal seams beneath you. The hump-backed moon shines close; damar tapped, frosted, caught vibrato in your throat, though you are not aware of making any sound.

It is becalmed here, not like the gusty air of the headland where you walked with Harry, through the shingle-hauled boats, spent carcasses sinking low on the tide.

Your tread ephemeral, ferns springing up behind you, the closing of a book before the final page.

Sequoia 12

The final page; early summer. The swelling in your ankles means you cannot pull on socks, fasten laces.

You sit. Then walk. Then sit. The trees eddying around you, a kaleidoscope of fairground rides; displaced circles of light, concentric tracks wild with celandine.

The beat of internal drums, the steroid-weight of your brain, the soft-flour heart of you,

at once

cold / feverish /
cold / with fever /
cold / pulsing
cold /

skin spidery with imagined crawlers; you, mittened and hatted despite the heat.

We used to know what we felt about all this: the wind, the heat, irrigation, the vast enclosures of managed forestry, the Christmas tree farms, running in lines to the sea; we used to agree on everything, Harry and I, how we could drizzle our lives into their spores, fortune-telling our directions, upwind and homesick for the future.

Now, there's blood on your ghost as it walks behind you.

Sequoia 13

Chances to die. There are many. Yours and sequoia's. The magician that vanishes the one from the other.

A vaulted room, the narrow flames of the rising sun; an open surge of starflowers in a rare clearing, a crossroads, each path doubling back on itself.

A heart deprived of blood, oxygen, beating in the box of your body; it's call to prayer—waking delirium, you sink down, taking it with you, a cupped butterfly in your tiny hands, honeying it back into sinus rhythm.

Some nights you are running beneath a clear, cold sky; and Harry,

Harry's far, far, behind you, a coda in your life, an apparition at every turn, his presence jack-knifing you back into your loss.

A heart carved here, two entwined there, girdling them—and you— into another story.

You rise up, look back to see if you are following.

Notes

We are all in this together. The Field of Reeds, as depicted in *The Egyptian Book of the Dead*, was the gateway to the afterlife. To reach it, the heart was weighed on a golden scale against a feather from the headdress of the Goddess Ma'at; if the heart was lighter than the feather, then the person's soul was considered 'sinless' and they could pass into The Field of Reeds; if it was heavier, it was thrown to the floor where it was eaten by Ammut, the female devourer of the dead.

CABG. Coronary artery bypass graft (CABG) is a surgical procedure used to treat coronary heart disease by creating new routes around narrowed and blocked arteries, permitting increased blood flow to deliver oxygen and nutrients to the heart muscle.

Matryoshka. John 19:34 records a legionnaire driving his spear through Christ's side and a flow of blood and water. Apparently Jesus was already dead (so his legs were not broken which was otherwise done to hasten death due to the body sagging under its own weight and causing internal drowning). As Christ was flogged before crucifixion, there would have been damage from the whip which contained weights and pieces of bone to flay the flesh. (The blood loss could be so severe that many people died at this stage.) This often caused low blood pressure, the kidneys shutting down to preserve fluid, and hypovolemic shock, which could lead to fluid gathering around the heart and lungs, and would explain the blood and water when the side was pierced, pointing to death by constriction of the heart due to the pressure of fluid.

Pumphead. A heart-lung machine or 'pump' takes over the function of the heart and lungs during the CABG surgery. Research suggests people on a heart-lung machine suffer from post-operative depression and cognitive failure.

The Berlin heart is a mechanical, pulsatile ventricular assist device (VAD) that mechanically supports the hearts of patients with end-stage heart failure, usually while they await transplant. The control unit and the two batteries are carried in a shoulder bag.

There are three hearts you can choose from. Surgeons can now use hearts in transplants that have stopped beating. The heart must be resuscitated by pumping warm oxygenated blood through the heart muscle, which means a donor heart can be maintained for up to 8 hours outside the body.

iota-eta-sigma. Bartolomeo Giuseppe Antonio Guarneri was an Italian luthier who rivalled Antonio Stradivari with regard to the respect and reverence accorded his instruments; he is known as *del Gesù* because his labels after 1731 incorporated the nomina sacra, I.H.S. (*iota-eta-sigma*).

Trick or treat. Researchers are genetically engineering pigs to carry a single human gene to produce human protein on the surface of their internal organs in the hope that this will trick the recipient's immune system into thinking the organ human, therefore avoiding hyperacute rejection. The first highly experimental pig-to-human heart transplant occurred in January 2022 at the University of Maryland School of Medicine, USA. The recipient died two months later, potentially due to a pig virus called porcine cytomegalovirus. As a result, researchers have developed more sensitive tests to screen donor organs for the virus.

Imago. An imago in psychoanalysis is an unconscious idealised mental image of someone which influences a person's behaviour; it is also the last stage of metamorphosis into the final fully-developed adult insect (typically winged).

Death hand. The death hand, a legendary 'cursed' poker hand, usually depicted as consisting of the ace of spades, ace of clubs, eight of spades and eight of clubs with an undefined fifth card, is thought to have been the hand which Wild Bill Hickok was holding when he was shot in the back of the head by Jack McCall on August 2, 1876, in Nuttal & Mann's Saloon at Deadwood, Dakota Territory.

A kicker, also called a side card, is a card in a poker hand that does not itself take part in determining the rank of the hand, but that may be used to break ties between hands of the same rank.

Foreign Body. 'Kiz Çocuğu' (The Little Girl) is an anti-war poem written in 1956 by Turkey's most important modern poet, Nazim Hikmet (1901-1963), who was persecuted and imprisoned for his outspoken Marxist views. The story is told by the ghost of a seven-year-old girl who died when the atomic bomb was dropped on Hiroshima.

sumi is a style of Japanese ink painting, or *sumi-e*, and is considered the embodiment of Japanese aesthetics. Using just simple black ink and carefully curated white space, *sumi-e* captures the timeless beauty and complexity of the natural world.

Takotsubo cardiomyopathy, or broken heart syndrome, is a weakening of the left ventricle, the heart's main pumping chamber, usually as the result of severe emotional or physical stress. It is characterised by transient left ventricular (LV) apical akinesis with hypercontraction of the basal wall creating a ballooning appearance of the heart which resembles the Japanese octopus trap, giving it its moniker, *Takotsubo*.

Sequoia 4. In Greek mythology, a *hamadryad* was a wood-nymph who was physically a part of her tree, who would die if her tree were felled.

Sequoia 9. Girdling—making a deep cut around the trunk of a tree—is a method of killing trees. Right below the bark are cells that transport a tree's food and water; slicing through these layers is the equivalent of disrupting the blood and oxygen supply in humans, causing the tree to decline or even starve to death.

www.ingramcontent.com/pod-product-compliance
Ingram Content Group UK Ltd.
Pitfield, Milton Keynes, MK11 3LW, UK
UKHW032350120525
458460UK00002B/93